FREEDOM
WALKERS

OTHER BOOKS BY RUSSELL FREEDMAN

Buffalo Hunt

Give Me Liberty!
The Story of the Declaration
of Independence

In Defense of Liberty
The Story of America's
Bill of Rights

Indian Chiefs

An Indian Winter

The Life and Death
of Crazy Horse

The Wright Brothers
How They Invented
the Airplane

FREEDOM WALKERS

The Story of the Montgomery Bus Boycott

→→→←←

RUSSELL FREEDMAN

→→→←←

HOLIDAY HOUSE / NEW YORK

Frontispiece: *Walking to work during the 381-day Montgomery bus boycott. Many boycotters walked hundreds of miles over the course of the year rather than ride the buses.*
Photo by Don Cravens/Getty Images

Copyright © 2006 by Russell Freedman
All Rights Reserved
Printed and Bound in July 2012 at Worzalla, Stevens Point, WI, USA.
Map by Heather Saunders
www.holidayhouse.com

7   9   10   8   6

Library of Congress Cataloging-in-Publication Data

Freedman, Russell.
Freedom walkers : the story of the Montgomery bus boycott /
Russell Freedman.— 1st ed.
p. cm.
Includes bibliographical references and index.
ISBN-13: 978-0-8234-2031-5 (hardcover)
ISBN-13: 978-0-8234-2195-4 (paperback)
1. African Americans—Civil rights—Alabama—
Montgomery—History—20th century—Juvenile literature.
2. African Americans—Alabama—Montgomery—
Biography—Juvenile literature.
3. Civil rights workers—Alabama—
Montgomery—Biography—Juvenile literature.
4. Segregation in transportation—Alabama—Montgomery—
History—20th century—Juvenile literature.
5. Montgomery (Ala.)—
Race relations—Juvenile literature.
6. Montgomery (Ala.)—Biography—
Juvenile literature. I. Title.
F334.M79N43 2006
323.1196'076'073071624—dc22
2006041148

＋＞＜＋

F O R K A T E

The warm and moving spirit
of Holiday House

＋＞＜＋

CONTENTS

Montgomery, Alabama, 1955–1956
Time of the Boycott

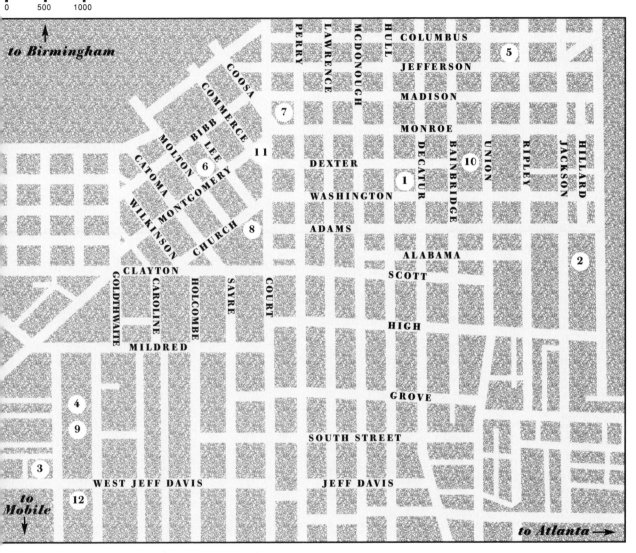

1 Dexter Avenue Baptist Church
2 Dexter Avenue Baptist Parsonage
  (home of Dr. Martin Luther King, Jr.)
3 Holt Street Baptist Church
4 Trinity Lutheran Church
5 First Baptist Church
6 Site of Rosa Parks's first arrest

7 City Recorder's Court
8 Courtroom
9 Rosa Parks's home
10 State Capitol
11 Court Square
12 E. D. Nixon's home

FREEDOM WALKERS

INTRODUCTION

WHY THEY WALKED

Not so long ago in Montgomery, Alabama, the color of your skin determined where you could sit on a public bus. If you happened to be an African American, you had to sit in the back of the bus, even if there were empty seats up front.

Back then, racial segregation was the rule throughout the American South. Strict laws—called "Jim Crow" laws—enforced a system of white supremacy that discriminated against blacks and kept them in their place as second-class citizens.

People were separated by race from the moment they were born in segregated hospitals until the day they were buried in segregated cemeteries. Blacks and whites did not attend the same schools, worship in the same churches, eat in the same restaurants, sleep in the same hotels, drink from the same water fountains, or sit together in the same movie theaters.

In Montgomery, it was against the law for a white person and a Negro to play checkers on public property or ride together in a taxi.

Most southern blacks were denied their right to vote. The biggest obstacle was the poll tax, a special tax that was required of all voters but was too costly for many blacks and for poor whites as well. Voters also had to pass a literacy test to prove that they could read, write, and understand the U.S. Constitution. These tests were often rigged to dis-

A segregated trolley car in Atlanta, Georgia, in 1956. Black and white passengers were separated by law on buses, trolleys, and trains throughout the South.
AP/Wide World Photos

qualify even highly educated blacks. Those who overcame the obstacles and insisted on registering as voters faced threats, harassment, and even physical violence. As a result, African Americans in the South could not express their grievances in the voting booth, which, for the most part, was closed to them. But there were other ways to protest, and one day a half century ago, the black citizens in Montgomery rose up in protest and united to demand their rights—by walking peacefully.

It all started on a bus.

ONE

JO ANN ROBINSON

"Get up from there!

Get up from there!"

Looking back, she remembered it as the most humiliating experience of her life, "a deep hurt that would not heal." It had happened just before Christmas in 1949. She was about to visit relatives in Cleveland, Ohio, where she would spend the holidays.

Earlier that day she had driven out to Dannelly Field, the Montgomery, Alabama, airport, and checked her luggage for the flight to Cleveland. Then she drove back to the campus of Alabama State, an all-black college where she had been hired that fall as a professor of English. After parking her car in the campus garage, she took her armful of Christmas gifts, walked to the nearest bus stop, and waited for a ride back to the airport.

Soon a Montgomery City Lines bus rolled into view and pulled up at the stop. Balancing her packages, Jo Ann Robinson stepped aboard and dropped her dime into the fare box. She saw that the bus was nearly empty. Only two other passengers were aboard—a black man in a

Jo Ann Robinson: "I think he wanted to hurt me, and he did."

seat near the back and a white woman in the third seat from the front. Without thinking, Robinson took a seat two rows behind the white woman.

"I took the fifth-row seat from the front and sat down," she recalled, "immediately closing my eyes and envisioning, in my mind's eye, the wonderful two-week vacation I would have with my family and friends in Ohio."

Jolted out of her reverie by an angry voice, she opened her eyes and sat upright. The bus driver had come to a full stop and turned in his seat. He was speaking to her. "If you can sit in the fifth row from the front seat of the other buses in Montgomery," he said, "suppose you get off and ride in one of them."

The driver's message didn't register at first. Robinson was still thinking about her holiday trip. Suddenly the driver rose from his seat, went over to her, and stood with his arm drawn back, as if to strike her. "Get up from there!" he yelled. "Get up from there!"

At the bus station in Durham, North Carolina, 1940
Library of Congress

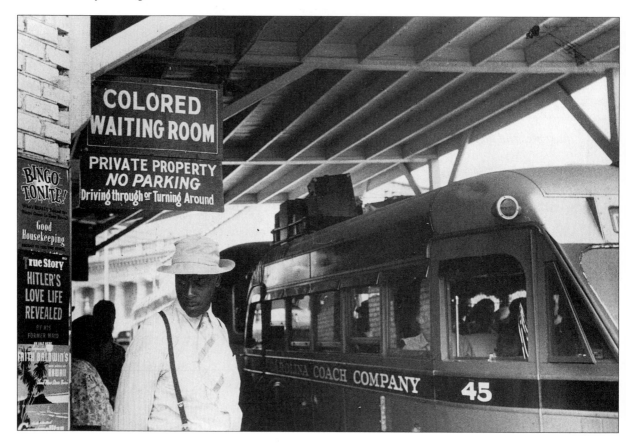

At the bus station in Memphis, Tennessee, 1943
Library of Congress

Shaken and alarmed, Robinson bolted to her feet and stumbled off
the bus in tears, packages falling from her arms. She had made the mis-
take of sitting in one of the front ten seats, which were reserved for
white riders only.

"I felt like a dog," she wrote later. "And I got mad, after this was over, and I realized I was a human being, and just as intelligent and far more [educationally] trained than that bus driver was. But I think he wanted to hurt me, and he did. . . . I cried all the way to Cleveland."

Robinson was still mad when she returned to Montgomery after the Christmas holidays. She had recently joined the local Women's Political Council (WPC), an influential organization of African American teachers, nurses, social workers, and other professional women who worked to advance black community interests. But when she told her fellow members what had happened, she learned that her experience was far from unusual. Scores of black passengers, mainly women, had suffered abuse from white bus drivers over the years. Such behavior was a fact of life in Montgomery, she was told. Members of the Women's Council had protested before, but it hadn't helped. Robinson made up her mind then that she would do everything in her power to challenge the city's segregated bus seating.

Every day, as many as 40,000 blacks rode Montgomery's public buses, along with some 12,000 whites. The first ten seats of every bus were reserved for white riders, with the last twenty-six available to blacks. But the dividing line between the white and black sections wasn't fixed. The driver had the power to expand the white section and shrink the black section by ordering blacks to give up their seats to whites.

As white passengers boarded the bus and dropped their dimes into the fare box, they took seats in the front. Black passengers were not allowed to walk past the white section after paying their fare. Instead, they had to get off the bus and reenter through the back door. Sometimes a spiteful driver would accept a black rider's fare and then, while the passenger was walking around to enter the back door, would drive off.

"Not all drivers were guilty of such practices," Robinson wrote. "There were some very fine, courteous bus drivers who were kindly disposed and carried out the laws of segregation without offending the riders. . . . There were good and mean drivers, considerate and hateful ones. And black riders had to cope with both types."

The bus system was a bitter daily reminder of enforced segregation in Montgomery. Many black riders were women who rode across town every morning to work as maids, cooks, and nurses in white homes. Other black passengers were students, young children, and old folks. All of them were powerless to challenge white drivers when they were ordered to give up their seats, because the drivers had the force of law behind them. Even when not a single white passenger was on board, the front ten seats in every bus were reserved for whites, just in case one or two did ride. Often black riders jammed the aisle of a bus, standing over those empty seats, where they dared not sit down. And if the white section happened to fill up, then the blacks sitting just behind the reserved seats had to get up as more whites got on. Elderly black men and women were required by law to get out of their seats so that white schoolchildren could take a seat.

Jo Ann Robinson did not take kindly to being pushed around. She had grown up on a small Georgia farm, the youngest of twelve children, had graduated from a segregated, all-black high school as the class valedictorian, and was the first member of her family to complete college. After teaching in Texas, she moved to Montgomery in the summer of 1949, at the age of thirty-seven, to join the English department at Alabama State, where she earned a reputation as an enthusiastic and popular teacher.

Robinson joined the Dexter Avenue Baptist Church, attended by many Alabama State professors. That's when she became a member of the Women's Political Council, which had been founded three years earlier when the local League of Women Voters refused to accept blacks. "We were 'woman power,' organized to cope with any injustice, no matter what," she recalled. "I had suffered the most humiliating experience of my life when that bus driver had ordered me off the fifth-row seat from the front and threatened to strike me when I did not move fast enough. Thus, I was ready to take over the WPC when the time came."

In 1950, she was elected president of the WPC. Under her leadership, segregated seating on public buses became the group's most pressing issue. Joined by other black community leaders, Robinson and the women of the WPC met several times with Montgomery city commissioners and, later, with bus company officials. Their demands were modest. They simply asked for "better seating arrangements." The word *integration* was never mentioned. "To admit that black Americans were seeking to integrate would have been too much," Robinson said later. "There probably would have been much bloodshed and arrests of those who dared to [suggest] such an idea!"

The black leaders complained about abusive drivers. They pointed out that bus stops were farther apart in black neighborhoods than in white areas. And they asked that the bus company hire some black drivers. The white officials listened politely. They reminded the blacks that segregation on public buses was required by both city and state laws. But

A segregated classroom at the University of Oklahoma, 1948. The black student, G. W. McLaurin, is seated in an anteroom, separated from white students.

Library of Congress

they did make a couple of small concessions. The mayor instructed the bus company to begin stopping at every corner in black neighborhoods, just as buses did in white sections of town. And he requested that drivers be more courteous in the future.

Nothing else changed. Then, on May 17, 1954, the *Montgomery Advertiser* carried a sensational front-page headline. In a momentous decision that would affect race relations across America, the United States Supreme Court had declared that segregation in the nation's public schools was unconstitutional. While the ruling had no immediate effect in Montgomery, many African Americans believed that the same principle applied to other segregated facilities, such as public transportation. Here at last was a real chance to challenge the segregation laws. Jo Ann Robinson was inspired to write to Montgomery Mayor W. A. "Tacky" Gayle, demanding improved conditions for black riders on city buses and mentioning, for the first time, the possibility of a boycott.

"Mayor Gayle, three-quarters of the riders on these public conveyances are Negroes," she wrote. "If Negroes did not patronize them they could not possibly operate. . . . There has been talk from twenty-five or more local organizations of planning a city-wide boycott of buses."

To be effective, a boycott would need the united support of the city's African American bus riders. Most of them could not afford to own automobiles. How would they get to work? Asking blacks to protest for their rights in the segregated South of the early 1950s was asking them to summon uncommon personal courage—to put their livelihoods and even their physical safety on the line. They could be fired from their jobs, harassed on the streets, or worse. The Ku Klux Klan and other white supremacy groups did everything they could to intimidate blacks into submission. And they did not shrink from violence. Blacks who broke the Jim Crow color bar might be terrorized, beaten, or even murdered.

"I did not have the slightest idea how—without involving others who might get hurt—to begin a boycott against the bus company," Robinson recalled.

But as stories continued to spread about abusive drivers and humiliating incidents on city buses, anger in the black community grew. The

Women's Political Council began to discuss plans for a boycott that would harness that anger and mobilize the strength of Montgomery's black community.

A masked Ku Klux Klansman holds a hangman's noose outside the window of a car as a warning during a Klan parade through an African American neighborhood in Miami, Florida, 1939.

Library of Congress

TWO

CLAUDETTE COLVIN

"It's my constitutional

right!"

Two youngsters from New Jersey—sixteen-year-old Edwina Johnson and her brother Marshall, who was fifteen—arrived in Montgomery to visit relatives during the summer of 1949. No one told them about the city's segregation laws for buses, and one day they boarded a bus and sat down by a white man and boy.

The white boy told Marshall to get up from the seat beside him. Marshall refused. Then the bus driver ordered the black teenagers to move, but they continued to sit where they were. Up North, they were accustomed to riding integrated buses and trains. They didn't see now why they should give up their seats.

The driver called the police, and Edwina and Marshall were arrested. Held in jail for two days, they were convicted at a court hearing of violating the city's segregation laws. Judge Wiley C. Hill threatened to send them to reform school until they were twenty-one, but relatives managed to get them an attorney. They were fined and sent back to New Jersey.

During the next few years, other black riders were arrested and convicted for the same offense—sitting in seats reserved for whites. They paid their fines quietly and continued to ride the public buses. It took a spunky fifteen-year-old high school student to bring matters to a head.

Claudette Colvin was an A student at all-black Booker T. Washington High. She must have been paying attention in her civics classes, for she insisted on applying the lessons she had learned after boarding a city bus on March 2, 1955.

Claudette was on her way home from school that day. She found a seat in the middle of the bus, behind the section reserved for whites. As more riders got on, the bus filled up until there were no empty seats left. The aisle was jammed with passengers standing, mostly blacks and a few whites.

The driver stopped the bus and ordered black passengers seated behind the white section to get up and move farther back, making more seats available for whites. Reluctantly, black riders gave up their seats and moved into the crowded aisle as whites took over the vacated seats.

Claudette Colvin: "I was just downright angry."
Montgomery Advertiser

Claudette didn't move. She knew she wasn't sitting in the restricted white section. She felt that she was far enough back to be entitled to her seat. A pregnant black woman was sitting next to her. When the driver insisted that the woman get up and stand in the aisle, a black man in the rear offered her his seat, then quickly left the bus to avoid trouble.

Claudette was now occupying a double seat alone. "Hey, get up!" the bus driver ordered. Still she refused to move. None of the white women standing would sit in the empty seat next to Claudette. It was against the law for blacks to sit in the same row as a white person.

The driver refused to move the bus. "This can't go on," he said. "I'm going to call the cops." He did, and when the police arrived, he demanded that Claudette be arrested.

"Aren't you going to get up?" one of the police officers asked.

"No," Claudette replied. "I don't have to get up. I paid my fare, so I don't have to get up." At school, Claudette had been studying the U.S. Constitution and the Bill of Rights, and she had taken those lessons to heart. "It's my constitutional right to sit here just as much as that [white] lady," she told the police. "It's my constitutional right!"

Blacks had been arrested before for talking back to white officials. Now it was Claudette's turn. She was crying and madder than ever when the police told her she was under arrest. "You have no right to do this," she protested. She struggled as they knocked her books aside, grabbed her wrists, and dragged her off the bus, and she screamed when they put on the handcuffs.

"I didn't know what was happening," she said later. "I was just angry. Like a teenager might be, I was just downright angry. It felt like I was helpless." She remained locked up at the city jail until she was bailed out later that day by the pastor of her church.

Under Montgomery's segregation laws, Claudette was in fact entitled to her seat behind the whites-only section. If no seats were available for blacks to move back to as additional white passengers boarded the bus, then they were not required to give up their seats. That was the official policy. But in actual practice, whenever a white person needed a seat, the driver would order blacks to get up and move to the back of the bus, even when they had to stand in the aisle.

Prosecutors threw the book at Claudette. She was charged not only with violating the segregation laws, but also with assault and battery for resisting arrest. "She insisted she was colored and just as good as white," the surprised arresting officer told the judge at the court hearing.

Claudette's arrest galvanized the black community. E. D. Nixon, an influential black leader, came to the teenager's defense. Nixon was employed as a

E. D. Nixon wanted to fight segregation in the federal courts.
Library of Congress

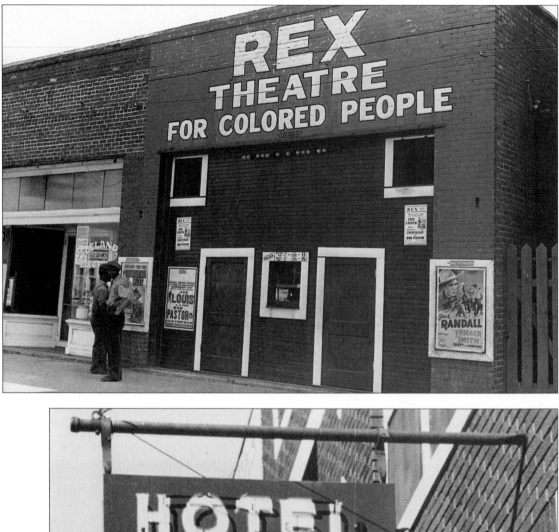

In the segregated South, strict Jim Crow laws required total separation of the races in almost every area of life. Even water fountains and vending machines were labeled for "whites" or for "colored" only.
Library of Congress

railroad sleeping car porter, but his passion was working to advance human rights. A rugged man with a forceful manner and a commanding voice, he had founded the Montgomery chapter of the National Association for the Advancement of Colored People (NAACP). Nixon was recognized by blacks and whites alike as a powerful presence in the black community, a vital force to be reckoned with. It was said that he knew every white policeman, judge, and government clerk in town, and he was always ready to help anyone in trouble.

When Nixon heard about Claudette Colvin's arrest, he got in touch with Clifford Durr, a liberal white attorney in Montgomery. Together they contacted Fred Gray, a twenty-four-year-old black lawyer who agreed to represent Colvin in court. Gray had grown up in Montgomery, attended Alabama State, and gone to Ohio for law school, because Alabama didn't have a law school for blacks. He was one of only two black attorneys in town.

After a brief trial in juvenile court, Claudette was found guilty of assault. She was fined and placed on probation in her parents' custody. She had expected to be cleared, and when the judge announced his verdict, she broke into agonized sobs that shook everyone in the crowded courtroom.

"The verdict was a bombshell!" Jo Ann Robinson recalled. "Blacks were as near a breaking point as they had ever been."

E. D. Nixon and other black leaders wanted to take the entire bus segregation issue into federal court. They hoped to demonstrate that segregated buses were illegal under the U.S. Constitution. But first they needed the strongest possible case—the arrest of a black rider who was above reproach, a person of unassailable character and reputation who could withstand the closest scrutiny. Claudette Colvin, Nixon felt, was too young and immature, too prone to emotional outbursts, to serve as standard-bearer for a long and expensive constitutional test case. As Nixon pointed out, she had fought with police, she came from the poorer side of black Montgomery, and it was later rumored that she was pregnant. "I had to be sure I had somebody I could win with . . . to ask people to give us a half million dollars to fight discrimination on a bus line," Nixon said later.

In October 1955, several months after Claudette was convicted, Mary Louise Smith, an eighteen-year-old black girl, was arrested when she refused to move to the back of the bus so a white woman could take her seat. "[The driver] asked me to move three times," Smith recalled. "And I refused. I told him, 'I am not going to move out of my seat. I am not going to move anywhere. I got the privilege to sit here like anybody else does.'"

Smith's case did not create the furor that the Colvin case did, because Smith chose to plead guilty. She was fined five dollars. Once

Mary Louise Smith in a photo taken years after her protest. "I am not going to move out of my seat," she told the bus driver.
Montgomery Advertiser

again, Nixon decided that Smith, like Colvin, wasn't the right person to inspire a battle against bus segregation.

Two months later, on December 1, 1955, another black woman boarded a city bus and found an empty seat just behind the white section. She was Rosa Parks.

THREE

ROSA PARKS

"The only tired I was,
was tired of giving in."

Rosa Parks had taken a special interest in Claudette Colvin's case. She knew Claudette. And she herself had suffered a similar experience twelve years earlier. In 1943, she had been thrown off a Montgomery bus for refusing to reenter through the back door after paying her fare. The bus driver had kept her money, ordered her to step outside, then driven away, leaving her standing on the sidewalk.

Parks worked as a seamstress in a downtown Montgomery department store, "where you had to be smiling and polite, no matter how rudely you were treated." A soft-spoken woman of forty-two, she wore rimless spectacles and had her brown hair braided and rolled behind her head. She was admired in the black community as a dedicated volunteer who had served as secretary of the local NAACP since 1943 and was currently an adviser to the organization's Youth Council, which counted Claudette Colvin among its members. Parks had been training

Rosa Parks at work as a seamstress
Photo by Don Cravens/Getty Images

her high school charges to resist segregation wherever they could. Recently, she had sent them to the whites-only public library to order books.

Rosa had grown up on a humble Alabama farm not far from Montgomery. "I was a field hand when I was quite young—not more than six or seven," she recalled. "I was given a flour sack like the other children and expected to collect one or two pounds of cotton."

Against great odds, Parks earned a high school diploma. At the time, Montgomery had no public high school for blacks. Rosa's family, ambitious for her advancement, arranged to send her to the laboratory school at Alabama State College, which trained black teachers. Rosa cleaned classrooms to help pay her way through school. After starting the eleventh grade, she had to drop out to care for her ailing grandmother, but she managed to return to school after she married. Rosa received her diploma when she was twenty years old, becoming one of a small number of black high school graduates in the city at that time.

"But that still didn't help me much in getting a job," she remembered. "I had a high school diploma, but I could only get jobs that didn't need a diploma." She worked in a shirt factory, as a helper in a hospital, and at a number of other menial jobs before being hired by the Montgomery Fair department store, where she altered ready-to-wear clothing.

Parks made extra money by taking in sewing on the side. She had done some work for Virginia Durr, wife of attorney Clifford Durr, and the two women became friends. The Durrs, a white couple, were known in Montgomery as outspoken equal rights activists. They thought so highly of Parks's civic activities that during the summer of 1955 they helped arrange a week's stay for Rosa at the Highlander Folk School in Monteagle, Tennessee, which held interracial workshops on how to promote integration. "That was the first time in my life I had lived in an atmosphere of complete equality with members of the other race," Parks said later. "I did enjoy going up there."

➤➤ ◄◄

On the evening of Thursday, December 1, 1955, Parks finished work and walked as usual to her regular bus stop at Court Square. Christmas lights were blinking in store windows, and people were hurrying home past a big banner that read PEACE ON EARTH, GOODWILL TO MEN.

As she boarded a bus and paid her fare, she recognized the driver

Rosa Parks (standing beside the brick column in a dark coat and hat) waits at a busy Montgomery bus stop. The Montgomery Fair department store, where she worked, is in the background.

Photo by Don Cravens/Getty Images

as the same man who had evicted her from his bus twelve years earlier. She found a seat in the middle section of the bus, behind the whites-only section. Three other black passengers boarded and sat next to Parks in the same row. Soon all thirty-six seats on the bus were filled, with twenty-two black passengers seated from the rear and fourteen white riders from the front.

Another white passenger boarded and stood in the aisle. The driver, James. P. Blake, turned in his seat to look behind him. He called to the first row of black passengers to stand up and move to the back. "Let me have those front seats," Blake ordered. All four passengers in the row would have to move so that the white man would not have to sit next to a black.

No one moved. Blake rose from the driver's seat and called out again: "Y'all better make it light on yourselves and let me have those seats." Reluctantly, three of the black passengers rose and moved to the back. Rosa Parks shifted slightly to allow the man next to her to get up, but she did not move from her seat. She wasn't sitting in the white section, and she didn't think that she should have to give up her seat and stand in the aisle the rest of the way home. She had just spent the entire day tailoring and pressing clothes for white folks.

Afterward, people would say that she didn't give up her seat because she was tired. "But that isn't true," she wrote later. "I was not tired physically, or no more tired than I usually was at the end of a working day. . . . No, the only tired I was, was tired of giving in." She had made up her mind long before that if she was ever asked to give up her seat for a white person, she would refuse.

"Look, woman, I told you I wanted the seat. Are you going to stand up?" the bus driver asked.

"No, I'm not," Parks replied.

"If you don't stand up, I'm going to call the police and have you arrested."

"You may do that," Parks replied, speaking so softly that Blake would not have been able to hear her if the bus engine had been running. Some of the black passengers, fearing trouble, started to get off the bus.

"As I sat there, I tried not to think about what might happen," Parks wrote. "I knew that anything was possible. I could be manhandled or beaten."

Soon, two Montgomery police officers arrived. Why hadn't she given up her seat? they asked. She felt she shouldn't have to, she told them. "Why do you all push us around?" she added. "I don't know," one policeman said, "but the law is the law, and you're under arrest."

Parks was escorted to a patrol car and driven to the city jail, where she was booked, fingerprinted, and photographed. Allowed one phone call, she called home. Her mother, who was living with her, answered. "I'm in jail," Rosa told her. "See if Parks [her husband] will come down here and get me out."

"Did they beat you?" her mother asked.

"No, I wasn't beaten, but I am in jail."

Parks's mother called E. D. Nixon, who had headed the local NAACP chapter when Rosa served as its secretary. Nixon tried to reach attorney Fred Gray, but he was out of town. After leaving a message for Gray, Nixon decided to call the jail himself. When he asked the desk ser-

Rosa Parks with E. D. Nixon (at left)

AP/Wide World Photos

geant about the charges against Rosa Parks, he was told that it was "none of his damned business."

Nixon then called Clifford Durr, who, as a white attorney, was able to get a civil answer from the desk sergeant. Parks had been charged with violating the state's segregation laws. Clifford and Virginia Durr then accompanied Nixon to the city jail, where they posted bond for Rosa and she was released.

"Mrs. Durr was the first person I saw as I came through the iron mesh door with matrons on either side of me," Parks recalled. "There were tears in her eyes, and she seemed shaken, probably wondering what they had done to me. As soon as they released me, she put her arms

Attorney Clifford Durr helped organize Rosa Parks's legal defense.
Library of Congress

around me, and hugged and kissed me as if we were sisters."

Later that night, at the Parkses' home, Rosa, her husband, Raymond, and her mother sat in the living room with Nixon and with Clifford and Virginia Durr as they discussed the details of her case and what to do about it. Nixon felt strongly that this was the test case he had been waiting for. Rosa was the ideal defendant. She had worked with Nixon for years at the NAACP, and he knew she was a person of exceptional dignity and strength of character. She possessed the quiet confidence to challenge the white establishment.

Nixon asked Rosa if she would be willing to fight the charges against her, to make her arrest a test case against segregated buses. "Mrs. Parks," he said, "with your permission we can break down segregation on the buses with your case." Rosa understood that this would be a momentous decision for herself and her family. Before agreeing, she wanted to speak privately with her mother and then with her husband.

Both of them were upset at first. Raymond, a barber at nearby Maxwell Air Force Base, knew that violence often awaited blacks who dared to challenge the system. "Oh, the white folks will kill you, Rosa," he warned. "Don't do anything to make trouble, Rosa. Don't bring a suit. The whites will kill you."

Racially motivated killings were not uncommon in the Jim Crow South. Early that year, two black men had been shot dead in Mississippi while trying to register African American voters. And that summer, in the small town of Money, Mississippi, fourteen-year-old Emmett Till, a black youngster visiting from Chicago, was kidnapped and beaten to death by a mob of Klansmen after he allegedly whistled at a white woman.

Emmett Till: His murder by white men during the summer of 1955 shocked the nation and helped galvanize the civil rights movement.
Library of Congress

Emmett's mutilated body, wrapped in barbed wire, was found floating in the Tallahatchie River. Montgomery newspapers had given prominent coverage to the brutal killing and the speedy trial of two white men accused of the crime, who were acquitted by an all-white jury. Several months later, the killers boasted to a journalist that they had indeed murdered Till.

Rosa Parks had not expected to resist on that December evening. And she did not want to put her family at risk. But she was no longer willing to accept the indignities of bus segregation, a system that dehumanized all black people. "I decided that I would have to know once and for all what rights I had as a human being and a citizen, even in Montgomery, Alabama."

After talking it over, Rosa's mother and husband said that they would support any decision she made. "If you think it will mean something to Montgomery and do some good, I'll be happy to go along with it," she told Nixon.

By now, it was late Thursday evening. Nixon and the Durrs left and went home. Attorney Fred Gray, meanwhile, had learned about Parks's arrest, had spoken with Rosa, and agreed to represent her. Then he called Jo Ann Robinson, whom he knew from the Claudette Colvin case, and Robinson, in turn, notified several fellow teachers who were members of the Women's Political Council. "It was all happening quickly," Gray recalled. "The mood was electric. This was the beginning of the Montgomery Bus Boycott."

At around midnight on December 1, the day Parks was arrested, Robinson and her friends met at their offices at Alabama State College, supposedly to grade last-minute exams. Actually, they were going to draft a letter of protest, calling on the black community to stage a one-day bus boycott on the following Monday, the date set for Parks's trial.

The fastest way to print copies of the letter was on the mimeograph machines at Alabama State (high-speed modern copy machines were still in the future). However, the college was funded by the state, and the teachers were state employees. If officials learned that they had used taxpayer-owned facilities to challenge the segregation laws, then funding for the all-black school might be cut back and the teachers might lose their jobs. The women swore one another to secrecy. They wrote and revised their letter, changing it repeatedly in the early hours of Friday morning. Then they stayed up the rest of the night cutting stencils and mimeographing 52,500 leaflets.

While the women were working, Robinson called Nixon at home to inform him of their plans for a boycott. He too had been busy throughout the night, phoning Montgomery's black ministers and other civic leaders, urging them to attend a meeting Friday evening to mobilize support for both the boycott and for the legal defense of Rosa Parks.

Early Friday morning, some students helped Robinson load leaflets into her car. She taught her classes from 8 A.M. to 10 A.M., then, accompanied by two senior students, set out to distribute the notices. Other Women's Council members were fanning out across town, doing the same thing. They stopped at black elementary, junior high, and high schools, where students were waiting to distribute the handbills in school so they could be taken home to parents. Leaflets were also dropped off at churches, stores, taverns, beauty parlors, barber shops, and every other available place. By the time the city's black ministers and civic leaders were ready to meet on Friday evening, thousands of anonymous notices had been circulated in Montgomery's black neighborhoods. Each leaflet read:

Another Negro woman has been arrested and thrown into jail because she refused to get up out of her seat on the bus for a white person to sit down. . . . If we do not do something to stop these arrests, they will continue. The next time it may be you, or your

This is for Monday, December 5, 1955

Another Negro woman has been arrested and thrown into jail because she refused to get up out of her seat on the bus for a white person to sit down.

It is the second time since the Claudette Colbert case that a Negro woman has been arrested for the same thing This has to be stopped.

Negroes have rights, too, for if Negroes did not ride the buses, they could not operate. Three-fourths of the riders are Negroes, yet we are arrested, or have to stand over empty seats. If we do not do something to stop these arrests, they will continue. The next time it may be you, or your daughter, or mother.

This woman's case will come up on Monday. We are, therefore, asking every Negro to stay off the buses Monday in protest of the arrest and trial. Don't ride the buses to work, to town, to school, or anywhere on Monday.

You can afford to stay out of school for one day if you have no other way to go except by bus.
You can also afford to stay out of town for one day. If you work, take a cab, or walk. But please, children and grown-ups, don't ride the bus at all on Monday. Please stay off of all buses Monday.

The typewritten text of the leaflet calling for a one-day bus boycott. More than fifty-two thousand copies were secretly run off on mimeograph machines at Alabama State and distributed in Montgomery's black neighborhoods.

daughter, or mother. This woman's case will come up on Monday. We are, therefore, asking every Negro to stay off the buses Monday in protest of the arrest and trial.

The leaflet urged the black community: "Don't ride the buses to work, to town, to school, or anywhere on Monday."

FOUR

MARTIN LUTHER KING, JR.

"I don't want anybody
to call me a coward."

The Reverend Martin Luther King, Jr., and his wife, Coretta, were up before dawn on the morning of Monday, December 5, 1955. Coretta sat at the living-room window, watching for the first morning bus to arrive at the bus stop just down the street. It was usually filled with black maids on their way to work.

Word of the boycott had been spreading through the city all that weekend. At their meeting on Friday evening, Montgomery's black ministers had drafted a leaflet of their own: "Don't ride the bus to work, to town, to school, or anywhere on Monday, Dec. 5. If you work, take a cab, or share a ride, or walk." And on Sunday, at every black church in town, preachers called on their congregations to support the protest.

No one knew if the boycott would be effective. Would Montgomery's black citizens unite and stay off the buses on that cold and overcast December morning? Or would they be intimidated by fears of white retaliation?

Martin Luther King, Jr., and Coretta Scott King with their infant daughter, Yoki, on the steps of the Dexter Avenue Baptist Church

Photo by Dan Weiner, courtesy of Sandra Weiner

At the Court Square bus shelter, a busy downtown stop, someone had posted a sign written on a piece of cardboard: PEOPLE DON'T RIDE THE BUSES TODAY. DON'T RIDE IT FOR FREEDOM.

"I was in the kitchen, drinking my coffee, when I heard Coretta cry, 'Martin, Martin, come quickly!'" King wrote later. "As I approached the front window, Coretta pointed joyfully to a slowly moving bus: 'Darling, it's empty!' I could hardly believe what I saw. I knew that the South Jackson line, which ran past our house, carried more Negro passengers than any other line in Montgomery."

One of many handwritten boycott posters placed at Montgomery bus stops: REMEMBER WE ARE FIGHTING FOR JUSTICE. DO NOT RIDE A BUS TODAY.

Another empty bus appeared, then another one. An excited King jumped into his car and drove around town for the next hour, peering at every passing bus. "By this time I was jubilant," he wrote. He knew now that the boycott was going to be a success.

King was twenty-six years old and a newcomer to Montgomery. He had moved to the city with Coretta the year before to take his first job as minister at the historic Dexter Avenue Baptist Church, which stood in the center of town across from the state capitol. He came from a family of eminent southern black preachers and civil rights activists. His father, Martin Luther King, Sr. (often called "Daddy King"), was pastor at the huge Ebenezer Baptist Church in Atlanta, which had been founded in 1894 by Martin Jr.'s maternal grandfather, A. D. Williams.

The first member of his family to be educated outside the South, Martin Jr. had earned a doctorate in theology at Boston University, where he had a reputation as a great dancer and a lively young man about town. He met Coretta Scott, a northern-educated, classically trained singer from Alabama, on a blind date and proposed to her soon afterward. King repre-

Buses ran nearly empty as the boycott began.
Photo by Dan Weiner, courtesy of Sandra Weiner

sented a new generation of African American leaders—highly educated young men who would rise to prominence through the ministry at a time when there were few black lawyers and when the usual political opportunities in city and state government were closed to blacks in the South.

That morning, the city's buses followed their usual runs carrying just handfuls of white passengers. Trailing many of the near-empty buses were pairs of white-helmeted motorcycle policemen, who had been assigned to "protect Negro riders." Police Commissioner Clyde Sellers had charged that "Negro goon squads" intended to threaten blacks who wanted to ride the buses. But the boycotters hadn't heard of any so-called "goon squads," and Sellers's plan backfired. "If there were any timid souls who would have ridden the bus despite the boycott, they

Motorcycle police watch a black-owned parking lot in Montgomery where boycotters are waiting for rides.

Photo by Don Cravens/Getty Images

were really frightened now," wrote Jo Ann Robinson. When these "faint-hearted few" saw heavily armed police trailing buses and keeping an eye on bus stops, they wanted no part of such a scene.

On almost every street corner in the downtown area, blacks stood waiting for taxi rides. E. D. Nixon had phoned each of Montgomery's eighteen black-owned taxi companies to ask for help. The companies had agreed to transport passengers for ten cents each, the same fare people would pay on the bus, rather than the usual forty-five-cent minimum for a cab ride. Every taxi was packed with people on their way to their jobs. Crowds of others were walking to work, bundled up against the cold, carrying their lunches in brown paper bags. Some boycotters walked more than twenty miles to and from work that day.

"The few Negroes who boarded buses," reported a local black historian, "found it difficult to get off without being embarrassed by other Negroes who waited [for taxis] at the bus stops throughout the city. Some were seen ducking in the aisles as the buses passed various stops."

Several hundred people greeted Rosa Parks when she arrived at court later that Monday morning. "The trial took all of ten minutes!" wrote Fred Gray, Parks's attorney. "The courtroom, of course, was segregated. I walked up the aisle, white people sitting on one side and black people on the other."

Found guilty of violating the segregation laws, Parks was given a suspended sentence and fined ten dollars plus four dollars in court fees—equivalent to 140 bus fares. Following her conviction, attorney Gray filed an appeal—the first step in the plan to challenge bus segregation in federal court.

Soon afterward, Parks lost her job at the Montgomery Fair department store. "They never said they fired her because of what she had done," Virginia Durr recalled. "What excuse [they gave] I don't know, but anyway, they fired her."

On the Monday afternoon following Parks's trial, Montgomery's black leaders met again to prepare for the big protest rally scheduled for that evening. It would be decided then whether to continue the bus boycott beyond its first day. When some of the preachers present balked at the idea of challenging Montgomery's powerful white establishment, E. D. Nixon lit into them. "Let me tell you gentlemen one thing," he began. "You ministers have lived off the sweat of these washerwomen for the last hundred years and ain't never done nothing for them. I am just ashamed of you." He scolded them for acting like cowards, for backing down like "little boys." "We've worn aprons all our lives," he continued. "It's time to take the aprons off. . . . If we're gonna be mens, now's the time to be mens."

King arrived at the meeting while Nixon was speaking, and he was the first to reply. "Brother Nixon, I'm not a coward," he said. "I don't want anybody to call me a coward."

After that, the meeting settled down. To help plan the boycott, the ministers agreed to form a new organization, the Montgomery Improvement Association (MIA). After some discussion, they elected King, the newcomer among them, as president of the group.

Until now, King hadn't played much of a role in community affairs. He'd wanted to concentrate on getting to know his parishioners and doing a good job at his first church. Recently he had turned down an invitation to head the local NAACP, and he did not seek the presidency of the new organization. "The [vote] caught me unawares," he wrote. "It happened so quickly I did not even have time to think it through. It is probable that if I had, I would have declined the nomination."

King was the unanimous choice to head the MIA. He had come out strongly in favor of the boycott. And he had demonstrated in his sermons that he was a powerful speaker. Since he hadn't been in town long and wasn't well known beyond his own church, he owed no obligations or debts to the city's black leadership or to its white establishment.

"Reverend King was a young man, a very intelligent young man," E. D. Nixon recalled. "He had not been here long enough for the city fathers to put their hand on him. Usually they'd find some young man

King speaks to a standing-room-only crowd at a boycott rally.

Photo by Dan Weiner, courtesy of Sandra Weiner

just come to town . . . pat him on the shoulder and tell him what a nice church he got. [They'd say,] 'Reverend, your suit don't look so nice to represent the so-and-so Baptist Church' . . . and they'd get him a suit. . . . You'd have to watch out for that kind of thing."

When the meeting broke up, King rushed home to prepare a speech for that night's mass rally. It would be his first appearance as the newly elected protest leader, and the first time most people in the audience would hear him speak.

King wanted to protest the injustices and inhumanities being inflicted on blacks. As a minister of the gospel, he also wished to express a vision of Christian charity that allowed him to love his fellow man. King had studied the teachings of Mahatma Gandhi and was inspired by the Indian leader's successful use of nonviolent resistance. Gandhi had united the people of India against the colonial rule of England by advocating nonviolence and passive resistance—that is, *refusing to cooperate with an unjust system.* "I had come to see early that the Christian doctrine of love operating through the Gandhian method of nonviolence was one of the most potent weapons available to the Negro in his struggle for freedom," King would later write. These were the thoughts that guided him as he quickly sketched an outline of his speech in his mind.

A friend drove King to the Holt Street Baptist Church, where the rally was being held. They had to park three blocks away and then push their way through the crowds. "The church itself holds four or five thousand people," Jo Ann Robinson recalled, "but there were thousands of people outside the church that night. They had to put up loudspeakers so they would know what was happening."

Joe Azbell, a reporter for the *Montgomery Advertiser,* also drove to
Holt Street, where he was to report on the rally. "The Holt Street Baptist
Church was probably the most fired up, enthusiastic gathering of human
beings that I've ever seen," he remembered. "I came down the street and
I couldn't believe there were that many cars. I parked many blocks from
the church just to get a place for my car. I went on up to the church, and
they made way for me because I was the first white person there.... I
was two minutes late and they were [already] preaching, and that audience was ... on fire.... The preacher would get up and say, 'Do you
want your freedom?' and they'd say, 'Yeah, I want my freedom!' ... I've
never heard singing like that.... They were on fire for freedom. There
was a spirit that no one could capture again.... It was so powerful.

"And then King stood up, and most of them didn't even know who
he was. And yet, he was a master speaker."

The speech that King was about to make would prove to be, he
recalled, "the most decisive of my life," launching his career as a leader
of the nation's civil rights movement. Yet he had little time to prepare
and had been "possessed by fear ... by a feeling of inadequacy." As he
stood at the pulpit that evening, without manuscript or notes, he looked
out upon a church jammed to the rafters. People packed the balcony,
stood shoulder-to-shoulder in the aisles, peered from outside through
the windows. They had gathered together as American citizens, King
began, "determined to apply our citizenship—to the fullness of its means."

King spoke in a deep, resonant voice, his words rolling out with a
pulsating rhythmic flow, then pausing as his audience responded with
murmured "Yeses" and "Amens." "But there comes a time," he cried, the

Waiting for rides at a car pool pickup station
Photo by Dan Weiner, courtesy of Sandra Weiner

FIVE

BOYCOTT HEROES

"My feets is tired,
but my soul is rested."

The boycott was still in its first week when Police Commissioner Clyde Sellers threatened to arrest any taxi driver who charged less than the minimum forty-five-cent fare. That meant that the so-called "taxicab army" with its emergency ten-cent-a-ride fare would no longer be available.

Dr. King phoned the Reverend T. J. Jemison, who had led a bus boycott in Baton Rouge, Louisiana, two years earlier. That boycott had lasted only a week, but it had resulted in a compromise agreement allowing black bus passengers to be seated on a first-come, first-served basis. Blacks would still have to begin their seating at the back of the bus, while whites would sit up front. Segregation would be preserved, but once seated, no one would have to give up a seat. While it was a small victory, the Baton Rouge boycott marked one of the first times an entire black community had organized and won a sustained direct action against segregation laws.

The lessons learned in Louisiana would now be put to use some four hundred miles away in Montgomery. To help transport people back and forth during the Baton Rouge boycott, Jemison had organized a massive car pool. King wanted to know exactly how that car pool worked. He grilled Jemison on every small detail. That very night, at a mass meeting in Montgomery, King told the crowd that they could do

Elected president of the Montgomery Improvement Association, King (at left) worked with the Transportation Committee to organize a massive car pool system.

Photo by Dan Weiner, courtesy of Sandra Weiner

the same. He called on car owners to volunteer their vehicles. And he urged those with licenses to volunteer as drivers.

In the black community, where relatively few people could afford a car, an automobile was a valued status symbol. Cars lent to the boycott would be used heavily, perhaps driven by strangers. To volunteer one's precious automobile as public transportation required an unwavering commitment to the boycott's success.

King announced that the city's black ministers would be willing to drive their own cars. After a pause, members of the audience began to raise their hands. Jo Ann Robinson volunteered to drive her car, the one she had used to deliver handbills announcing the boycott. Mrs. A. W. West stood and offered her green Cadillac. More hands went up. That first night, more than 150 people signed up to lend their cars to the boycott.

To be effective, the car pool had to be planned and executed as precisely as a military campaign. An intricate web of pickup and drop-off points was needed, along with a communications system that would connect those needing rides with those offering them. The MIA set up a Transportation Committee headed by Rufus Lewis, a successful businessman, a former college football coach at Alabama State, and a pioneer in voter registration. Lewis recruited some black postal workers who knew the layout of the city's streets, and they developed an interlocking system of forty-eight dispatch and forty-two pickup stations.

During the weeks that followed, people continued to offer their cars or volunteer as drivers. Eventually between 275 and 300 black-owned vehicles were transporting thousands of boycotters every day. Thousands more people were walking to work, to school, to the store, or wherever they had to go. Many of the boycotters worked for white employers as housemaids or day laborers, often the only jobs available to them. Despite rainstorms, freezing winter mornings, mechanical breakdowns, and scheduling snafus, they managed to get from home to job and then home again, with the help of the car pool or on foot.

To bolster morale and keep the boycotters informed, mass meetings were held every Monday and Thursday evening at black churches scattered around town, so that folks would not have to walk too far. These meetings became popular community events, often attended by two thousand boycotters or more. People would start to arrive at three or four in the afternoon, bringing their dinners with them, so they could get good seats for the meeting starting at seven.

At each meeting, speakers would single out certain walkers and praise them as boycott heroes. One minister told the crowd about an elderly woman who vowed that if her feet gave out, she would crawl on her knees before boarding a bus. Another preacher described a group of women he had seen walking to work one morning. They were carrying themselves with pride and dignity, he said, in a manner that would "do justice to any queen."

Moved by the spirit of the occasion, people would rise from their seats, make their way to the front of the church, and offer some personal testimony of their support for the cause. One elderly woman, known to everyone as Mother Pollard, had refused a ride from a car-owning minister. When he suggested politely that she could drop out of the boycott because of her age, she said that she preferred to walk. She could walk along with the best of them, she insisted. "My feets is tired, but my soul

Boycott leaders: Attorney Fred Gray (left), the Reverend Ralph Abernathy (center), and the Reverend Robert Graetz
AP/Wide World Photos

is rested," Mother Pollard announced with uncertain grammar but memorable eloquence—a spontaneous remark that folks delighted in repeating. Passed from mouth to mouth, it became a familiar refrain of the protest movement.

Car pool passengers could not pay directly for their rides—that would violate the city's taxi regulations—but they could make contributions to the MIA, and they did. "This movement was made up of just ordinary black people, some of whom made as little as five dollars a week," reporter Joe Azbell recalled. "But they would give a dollar of that to help support the boycott."

As news of the boycott spread, money began to pour in from outside sources. The protest was becoming a big story in newspapers across the country and on television newscasts, and the longer the boycott lasted, the bigger the story became. The NAACP organized fund-raising events, and sympathizers from both the North and South sent contributions to support the Montgomery Improvement Association's transportation network. Eventually, the MIA was able to buy some thirty cars of its own, mainly station wagons. Various churches had their names painted on the sides of many of these cars, which became known as "rolling churches."

As the boycott continued, black leaders met with white officials in several attempts to reach a compromise agreement. The boycotters were not demanding an end to segregated seating on the buses. "That's a matter for the legislature and the courts," said King. "We feel we have a plan within the [existing] law." They had three demands:

1) Courteous treatment on the buses.
2) Hiring of black drivers on routes serving black neighborhoods.
3) First-come, first-served seating by race, blacks from the back of the bus and whites from the front until all seats were taken. With that arrangement, blacks would no longer have to give up their seats for whites or stand over empty seats.

"We will certainly be willing to guarantee courtesy," said bus company attorney Jack Crenshaw, but he insisted that most drivers were, in fact, courteous. He rejected the demand for black drivers, arguing that blacks did not have the right to tell the company whom to hire. "We have no intention now or in the foreseeable future of hiring 'niggras,'" Crenshaw said.

As for the main demand—bus seating—Crenshaw claimed that the boycotters' plan would be illegal under existing segregation laws. "If it were legal I would be the first to go along with it, but it just isn't legal," he said.

Fred Gray, attorney for the black delegation, disagreed. He pointed out that a first-come, first-served seating arrangement was already in practice in some other southern cities. The boycotters' requests "were not designed to integrate the buses," Gray emphasized. "Rather they were intended as very reasonable reforms. The city officials could have given in to us but they simply refused."

Attorney Crenshaw wouldn't budge. "If we grant the Negroes these demands," he finally said, "they would go about boasting of a victory that they had won over the white people, and this we will not stand for."

"I left the meeting despondent," King wrote later. "Feeling that our demands were moderate, I had assumed that they would be granted with little question. This experience, however, taught me a lesson. . . . I saw that the underlying purpose of segregation was to oppress and exploit the segregated, not simply to keep them apart. Even when we asked for justice *within* the segregation laws, the 'powers that be' were not willing to grant it. Justice and equality, I saw, would never come while segregation remained, because the basic purpose of segregation was to perpetuate injustice and inequality."

Within a month, the bus company warned that it was losing money and asked permission to double the fare from ten to twenty cents. It was granted a five-cent raise. White riders were not even beginning to make up for the loss of black passengers. The mayor urged whites to ride the buses. So did the White Citizens Council, an organization of prominent businessmen and politicians dedicated to maintaining racial segregation. But most whites drove cars and could not bring themselves to climb aboard a public bus.

A small number of local whites openly supported the boycott. "Our 'share-a-ride' slogan received a wonderful response," Jo Ann Robinson reported. "Sympathetic whites, both men and women, stopped and picked up pedestrians. Young white drivers would stop and allow walkers to 'pile in.'"

The Reverend Robert Graetz, the white pastor of Trinity Lutheran, a black church, had announced from the pulpit that he and his family would observe the boycott, and he urged everyone in his congregation to do the same. With a handful of other white liberals, Graetz was a member of the Montgomery Human Relations Council. At first, segregationists suspected that Graetz himself was the organizer of the boycott.

Juliette Morgan, a white librarian and another member of the Human Relations Council, wrote to the *Montgomery Advertiser*, comparing the bus boycott to Mahatma Gandhi's struggle against British rule in India. "It is hard to imagine a soul so dead, a heart so hard, a vision so blinded and provincial as not to be moved with admiration at the quiet dignity, discipline, and dedication with which the Negroes have conducted their boycott," Morgan wrote. "One feels that history is being made in Montgomery these days." After her letter appeared, rocks were thrown through the windows of her house, she received threatening phone calls, and she was insulted on the street.

Montgomery's city officials weren't sure how they should deal with the black community's united display of nonviolent resistance to segregation. Segregationists were demanding that the city get tough. "I hope the Negroes walk until they get bunions and blisters," one man told reporter Joe Azbell.

As the boycott continued through Christmas and into the new year of 1956, Mayor Gayle and his fellow city commissioners made a dramatic show of joining the White Citizens Council. And they attacked King personally, calling him a troublesome outsider who had never even been on a city bus in Montgomery.

Robert Graetz was the white pastor of Trinity Lutheran, a church with an all-black congregation.
Photo by Dan Weiner, courtesy of Sandra Weiner

A meeting of the White Citizens Council. Its members supported harsh economic reprisals against blacks who fought segregation.

Photo by Dan Weiner, courtesy of Sandra Weiner

SIX

PROUD TO BE ARRESTED

"I say, let's all go to jail!"

Tensions were rising in Montgomery. In January, the bus company announced that it was on the verge of bankruptcy. Downtown businesses, lacking customers, also were suffering heavy losses. Telegrams, phone calls, and letters poured into City Hall, urging the mayor to put an end to the boycott and hold the line against integration.

Mayor Gayle had enjoyed a favorable reputation in the black community, "a very pleasant person," according to Jo Ann Robinson, "very likeable, easy to approach, and sincere in working with us." But now the mayor was under fire. Facing increasing pressure from hard-line segregationists, he announced that he would no longer negotiate.

"There seems to be a belief on the part of the Negroes that they have the white people hemmed up in a corner," the mayor said, "and they are not going to give an inch until they can force the white community to submit to their demands—in fact, swallow all of them. . . . There is

An African American motorist gets a ticket during a police crackdown on car pool drivers.

Photo by Don Cravens/Getty Images

Montgomery Mayor W. A. "Tacky" Gayle joined the White Citizens Council and announced a get-tough policy against boycotters.

AP/Wide World Photos

no need for us to straddle the fence any longer. I am taking a stand and so are the other city commissioners."

The mayor was upset that a lot of white women were driving their black housekeepers and cooks to and from work every day. He appealed to the white employers not to support the boycott in that way, but for the most part, his pleas were ignored. "If the mayor wants to come and do my washing and ironing and look after my children and clean my house and cook my meals, he can do it," said one woman. "But I'm not getting rid of my maid."

The city commissioners were convinced that most blacks wanted to ride the buses but were being tricked and manipulated by the boycott leaders, "a group of Negro radicals," the mayor called them. He singled out King as the ringleader. The way to end the boycott, the commissioners agreed, was to frighten or discredit King and his fellow black leaders.

Police Commissioner Sellers ordered his men to crack down on the car pool drivers. Officers began to stop cars and question drivers about their licenses, their insurance, their place of work. They checked headlights, taillights, and windshield wipers, and wrote tickets for minor and sometimes imaginary violations. People who had never in their lives received a traffic ticket were booked and at times taken to jail. Jo Ann

Many of the boycotters were black housekeepers, nurses, and cooks who worked for white families.

Photo by Dan Weiner, courtesy of Sandra Weiner

Robinson, a stickler for obeying traffic rules, received seventeen tickets over a period of two months, some for going too fast, others for driving too slow. Police also harassed boycotters who were waiting at pickup stations for rides. They were warned that there was a law against hitch-hiking; some were told they'd be arrested for vagrancy if they did not move on.

On January 26, 1956, King himself was pulled over by two motorcycle policemen while transporting three boycotters he had picked up at a car pool station. "Get out, King," one of the officers ordered. "You're under arrest for speeding thirty miles an hour in a twenty-five-mile zone." King did not attempt to argue. When he stepped out of his car, he was searched. Then he was put into the back of a radio-summoned patrol car and driven to the city jail, where he was booked, fingerprinted, and taken to a crowded cell. "All right, get in there with the others," his jailer said.

Among the other prisoners—drunks, vagrants, and petty criminals—he recognized two acquaintances, one a respected schoolteacher, who had also been arrested as car pool drivers. "For the first time in my life," he recalled, "I had been thrown behind bars."

As word of King's arrest spread, his supporters began to gather at the city jail. The police had expected to hold him overnight, but as the crowd of blacks outside the jailhouse grew bigger and noisier, King was abruptly taken from his cell, released on his own recognizance (without bail), and ushered out the front door of the jail, where he was greeted by a jubilant throng of friends and well-wishers. That night, mass meetings were held at several black churches to protest his arrest.

At King's home, meanwhile, he had been receiving threatening letters and phone calls. Postcards signed "KKK" [Ku Klux Klan] advised him to "get out of town or else." Often the phone would ring, and when King or Coretta answered, the caller at the other end would simply hang up. Other callers shouted insults and obscenities at anyone who answered. "Listen, nigger," one caller warned, "we've taken all we want from you. Before next week you'll be sorry you ever came to Montgomery."

At first, King took the threatening calls and letters in stride, dismissing them as the work of a few hotheads. But as the weeks passed, he began to realize "that many of the threats were in earnest. Soon I felt myself faltering and growing in fear. One day, a white friend told me that he heard from reliable sources that plans were being made to take my life. For the first time I realized that something could happen to me."

As King wrote later, he was able to overcome his fears and find the courage to continue as he sat worried and exhausted at his kitchen table early one morning, his cup of coffee untouched before him. "With my head in my hands, I bowed over the table and prayed aloud. . . . Almost at once my fears began to go. My uncertainty disappeared. I was ready to face anything."

Three nights later, on January 31, King was speaking at a mass meeting when he was pulled aside and told that someone had hurled a homemade bomb through a window of his house. He rushed home. A crowd of angry black men, women, and children, some of them brandishing guns, knives, or broken soda bottles, were milling about outside the house. The police were shouting at them to disperse. The air smelled of dynamite. Broken glass littered the front porch. Inside, the living and dining rooms were crowded with members of King's congregation and

Volunteer sentinels and floodlights guard the King family home after a bomb was thrown through a front window.

Photo by Dan Weiner, courtesy of Sandra Weiner

with some first-time visitors to the King home—Mayor Gayle, Police Commissioner Sellers, the fire chief, and several white reporters.

King brushed past them into a bedroom and embraced his wife. Coretta and their ten-week-old daughter, Yoki, had been in back of the house with a friend when the bomb went off. None of them had been injured.

Reassured that his family was safe, King went back to the dining room to speak to the mayor and the police commissioner. Both men condemned the bombing. They promised to do everything possible to catch the people responsible. And they expressed regret that "this unfortunate incident has taken place in our city."

Then a trustee of King's church spoke up. It was C. T. Smiley, the principal of all-black Booker T. Washington High School. His livelihood depended on the goodwill of the city fathers, but even so, he turned to the police commissioner and said, "Regrets are fine, Mr. Sellers, but you must face the fact that your public statements created the atmosphere for this bombing. This is the result of your 'get-tough' policy." Neither the mayor nor the police chief replied.

King went out to the front porch, raised his hand for silence, and asked everyone to go home peacefully. "Let's not get panicky," he told them. "If you have weapons, take them home. If you do not have them, please do not seek to get them. . . . Remember, we are not advocating violence. . . . We must meet hate with love."

When the police commissioner stepped forward to speak, the crowd booed him. King raised his hand again, asking for silence. "Let us hear the commissioner," he said. Sellers offered a reward to anyone who could identify the person or persons who had set off the bomb. And he promised full police protection for the King family. When he finished speaking, the crowd broke up and began to drift home.

Two nights later, a stick of dynamite was thrown onto the lawn in front of E. D. Nixon's house. Again, no one was hurt. And while another angry crowd gathered at the house, they too were persuaded to go home peacefully. "Nonviolence had won its first and second tests," King wrote. At mass meetings, he had repeatedly emphasized the power of nonviolent resistance.

Even so, King's friends decided that it was too dangerous for him to drive any longer or even to travel alone. To protect him, they organized a volunteer corps of drivers and bodyguards, and they had floodlights installed around his house for security.

Jo Ann Robinson also became a target. One night a big stone was thrown through the picture window of her house. Two weeks later, acid was scattered over her parked car, burning holes on the roof, fenders, and hood. "I kept that car, a Chrysler, until 1960," she said. "It had become the most beautiful car in the world to me."

Matters came to a head when a Montgomery judge impaneled a special grand jury made up of seventeen whites and one black to investigate racial unrest in the city. More than 200 witnesses were summoned to testify about who was leading the boycott. On February 21, the grand jury indicted 115 blacks—including King, 23 other ministers, and all the car pool drivers—under an obscure 1921 state law prohibiting boycotts "without just cause or legal excuse."

The city commissioners issued an ultimatum: If the boycotters accepted the settlement terms they had previously rejected, charges against them would be dropped. The offer was turned down. "We have walked for eleven weeks in the cold and rain," the Reverend Ralph Abernathy told reporters. "Now the weather is warming up. Therefore we will walk on until some better proposals are forthcoming from our city fathers."

When the indictments were announced, King was out of town, lec-

Defendants and their supporters jam the Montgomery courthouse after a grand jury indicted 115 boycotters, including twenty-four ministers.

AP/Wide World Photos

turing at Fisk University in Nashville, Tennessee. Abernathy phoned to inform him. In Montgomery, Abernathy reported, many of the indicted boycott leaders were planning to show their defiance by giving themselves up in groups, rather than waiting to be arrested. "I say, let's all go to jail!" the Reverend S. S. Seay declared.

King told Abernathy he would return to Montgomery right away. He made reservations to fly back by way of Atlanta, where Coretta and the baby were visiting his parents. When he arrived in Atlanta, his father met him at the airport and pleaded with him not to go back to Montgomery. In the past, Martin Luther King, Sr., had been an outspoken campaigner for civil rights, but now he was terrified at what might happen to his son and his family. "They are out to get you," the elder King warned. He asked several trusted family friends to come to the house that afternoon and talk to his son.

King, Jr., agreed to meet with them, but he had made up his mind. "I must go back to Montgomery," he told them. "It would be the height of cowardice for me to stay away." With that, his father broke down. "They're going to kill my boy," he sobbed. But when the others spoke up to support the younger King's decision, Daddy King recovered his composure and vowed that he would stick by his son. He intended to accompany Martin back to Montgomery.

In Montgomery, meanwhile, most boycotters didn't wait for the sheriff's deputies to come after them. E. D. Nixon was the first to be arrested. He walked into the county courthouse, entered the sheriff's office, and asked, "Are you looking for me? Well, here I am." Taken by surprise, the sheriff's deputies welcomed him to jail. He was booked,

Rosa Parks was one of those arrested and booked for boycotting without "a just cause or legal excuse." This was her second arrest.

AP/Wide World Photos

fingerprinted, photographed, and quickly released on bond. He walked out of the courthouse smiling.

Word spread, setting off a chain reaction as more indicted boycotters showed up voluntarily at the courthouse. Among those who were arrested, booked, and then released were Jo Ann Robinson and a fellow member of the Women's Political Council, Irene West, who was nearly eighty years old. Another senior was Dr. M. C. Cleveland, pastor of the Day

Street Baptist Church. "This is the first time I have been arrested for anything in seventy-two years," he said. "This is a new experience, but at my age you are used to new experiences."

Hundreds of spectators gathered outside the jailhouse, shouting encouragement as the boycotters walked inside to be booked, cheering and applauding when they left. The act of being arrested, which for so long had terrified the black community, had become a badge of honor. People who had once trembled before the law were now proud to be arrested for the cause of freedom. As the exuberant crowd of onlookers laughed and cheered, waving and hugging boycott leaders as they passed in and out, some of the white sheriff's deputies began to enjoy themselves too, laughing and trading jokes with the crowd, until the sheriff himself stormed outside to shout, "This is no vaudeville show!"

"It became a real honor to have been indicted and arrested," Fred Gray recalled. "Any number of persons who were not indicted were very disappointed. . . . They felt they had been somewhat insulted by not having been arrested for exercising their constitutional rights."

When King arrived in Montgomery the next morning, he headed immediately for the county courthouse, accompanied by his father, Ralph Abernathy, and several members of his congregation. The crowd waiting for them cheered when they arrived. King was booked, fingerprinted, and photographed, as he had been once before. Then he was released into the waiting arms of his supporters. He was the twenty-fourth minister to be arrested. His trial was set for March 19.

While all this was happening, the black leadership had voted to move forward with their legal strategy. On February 1, after King's

Montgomery Sheriff's Department booking photos of Rosa Parks and Martin Luther King, Jr. All those arrested were booked, fingerprinted, photographed, and released on bond.
AP/Wide World Photos

house was bombed, attorney Fred Gray had filed papers in federal court challenging bus segregation as a violation of the United States Constitution. By that time, Gray's appeal of Rosa Parks's case had been thrown out on a technicality; her conviction had been upheld. "The new suit was our way of getting tough," Parks wrote. This time, it was filed on behalf of five women who had been mistreated on the buses, among them Claudette Colvin and Mary Louise Smith.

Everyone knew that it might take months, if not years, to resolve the lawsuit. Ultimately, the U.S. Supreme Court would have to decide. Until then, the boycott, now in its fifty-ninth day, would continue. The black citizens of Montgomery would just have to keep on walking.

The Reverend Ralph Abernathy hugs a supporter outside the courthouse after being arrested for participating in the bus boycott.
AP/Wide World Photos

Walking to work instead of riding the bus

Photo by Don Cravens/Getty Images

SEVEN

WALKING TO VICTORY

*"We are glad to have
you this morning."*

The city commissioners had expected to break the spirit of the boycott. But the mass arrests, far from delivering a crushing blow, inspired the boycotters and strengthened their resolve. *Montgomery Advertiser* editor Grover Hall called the wholesale indictments and arrests "the dumbest act that has ever been done in Montgomery."

On the evening after King was booked and released, thousands of people crowded into a mass meeting at Ralph Abernathy's church. All of the men and women who had been arrested so far assembled at the front of the church as the members of the audience rose to their feet, cheering and applauding, bringing their children forward to reach out and touch the boycott heroes. Abernathy called for a day of thanks—a day when everyone would walk. There would be no car pool, no private cars, no taxis. Boycotters "would not turn a key in the switch, nor touch a starter, nor take a cab, but would walk everywhere . . . so that those who walked would know that others walked with them."

City officials had "revealed that they did not know the Negroes with whom they were dealing," King wrote. "They thought they were dealing with a group that could be cajoled or forced to do whatever the white man wanted them to do. They were not aware that they were dealing with Negroes who had been freed from fear."

By now, scores of newspaper and television reporters had descended on Montgomery from all over the United States and Europe, from as far

A cheering, waving crowd greets boycott leaders during a mass meeting at Ralph Abernathy's church, crowded with black boycotters as well as white reporters and TV crews.
AP/Wide World Photos

away as Japan, India, and Australia. The boycott, the bombings, and the arrests had become a major international news story. The world was waiting to see what would happen.

King's trial opened on March 19, 1956. He had been singled out by prosecutors as a test case in their plan to declare the boycott illegal and to punish its leaders. Trials of the other indicted boycotters had been set aside for the time being. The NAACP had sent lawyers to help with King's defense, but the outcome in that Montgomery courtroom was never really in doubt. King was found guilty. He was sentenced to pay a five-hundred-dollar fine or serve a year at hard labor. Judge Eugene Carter said he had imposed a "minimum" sentence because of what King had done to prevent violence.

"I came to the end of my trial with a feeling of sympathy for Judge Carter," King recalled. "To convict me, he had to face the condemnation of the nation and world opinion. To acquit me, he had to face the condemnation of the local community and those voters who kept him in office. Throughout the proceedings he had treated me with great courtesy, and he rendered a verdict which he probably thought was the best way out."

Released on bond, King left the courthouse with his wife at his side and a host of friends following. Outside, he was greeted by television cameramen and news photographers, and by hundreds of supporters who shouted "God bless you!" and began to sing, "We ain't gonna ride the buses no more."

The NAACP announced that its lawyers would represent King in his appeal, as well as any other boycott leaders brought to trial. NAACP

King is welcomed with a kiss by his wife, Coretta, after leaving the Montgomery courtroom where he was found guilty of leading an "illegal" boycott. Attorney Fred Gray looks on from behind Coretta at left.

attorneys were also backing Fred Gray in his federal suit challenging bus segregation. A number of influential whites tried to persuade Gray to drop the case. "Some suggested that I dismiss the case outright because it would only create problems in the community and give me the reputation of an agitator," Gray wrote later. "Some officials suggested that if I would get my clients to agree to either dismiss the case or have it passed over, I would not have to worry, and they would assure me that from that point forward I would have all the legal cases I could handle. Of course, I never would have agreed to such an inducement."

Early that summer, the boycotters won their first legal victory. On June 4, a special three-judge federal court ruled in favor of the boycott leaders. By a two-to-one vote, the white southern judges declared that Alabama's state and local laws requiring segregation on buses violated the Fourteenth Amendment to the U.S. Constitution, which guarantees equal protection under the law. Segregation on city buses was declared unconstitutional.

Attorneys for Montgomery and for the state of Alabama immediately appealed the ruling to the U.S. Supreme Court. For the time being, the segregation laws remained in force. Several months would pass before the Supreme Court could hand down its decision.

"The battle was not yet won," King wrote. "We would have to walk and sacrifice for several more months, while the city appealed the case."

The bus protest continued. Montgomery's black citizens had been walking and carpooling for six months now. There had been some fifty mass meetings to keep up morale, a dozen bombings, and hundreds of arrests. Boycotters had been threatened, harassed, and fired from their jobs. But the June court ruling was greeted with rejoicing and with a renewed sense of optimism. At long last, a court had upheld the protesters' cause. The first six months had been the hardest, everyone agreed; they would keep on walking for another six months if they had to. "We were not even tired," Fred Gray recalled.

Seven-year-old Bernice Robertson and her sisters, Rosetta, nine, and Naomi, ten, clearly weren't tired. Since the first week of the boycott, they had walked more than eight miles a day, twice a week, just to take piano lessons. "We walked because it was right and because it was wrong to get on the bus," Bernice remembered. "And it wasn't easy, either . . . because sometimes white folks would go by and blow the horn or yell things at us, because they knew what we were a part of, what we were doing."

In August, there was another bombing. This time the target was the home of Robert Graetz, the white minister who had openly supported the bus boycott. Three sticks of dynamite exploded in Graetz's front yard with enough force to shatter windows in nearby homes. Again, no one was hurt. Mayor Gayle charged that Graetz might have bombed his own house in order to encourage out-of-state contributions to the MIA. "Perhaps this is just a publicity stunt to build up interest of the Negroes in their campaign," the mayor told reporters.

That autumn, the White Citizens Council tried to cripple the boy-cotters' car pool by preventing the MIA's fleet of station wagons, the "rolling churches," from getting insurance coverage. Insurance agents throughout the South were pressured to cancel the fleet's liability insur-ance. Without such insurance, car pool vehicles could not operate legally. King finally arranged for new insurance through a black agent in Atlanta, who was able to buy a policy from Lloyd's of London, a British firm. The car pool continued to roll. Blacks had stayed off the buses all summer and into the fall.

The segregationists did not give up. City officials asked a state court for an injunction banning the car pool as an unlicensed municipal trans-

Car pool station wagons sponsored by church congregations were known as "rolling churches."
Montgomery Advertiser

portation system. If the court agreed, then anyone who continued to operate the car pool could be jailed for contempt. A hearing on the injunction was set for November 13.

The night before the hearing, King went before a mass meeting to warn that the car pool would probably be outlawed. After nearly twelve months, the boycotters would lose their only means of transportation other than walking. Could they persist with the car pool destroyed? Could their leaders ask everyone to walk back and forth every day to their jobs, no matter how far? For the first time, King felt the cold wind of pessimism passing through the audience. And as the meeting broke up, people walked home silently, under a cloud of uncertainty.

On Tuesday, November 13, King and his fellow boycott leaders sat glumly in a Montgomery courtroom as lawyers for the city argued that the car pool should be banned and the MIA fined heavily for operating an unlicensed transportation service. During a brief recess, King noticed an unusual commotion. Mayor Gayle and Police Commissioner Sellers

Martin Luther King, Jr., (at left) and Ralph Abernathy arrive at the Montgomery courthouse.
AP/Wide World Photos

were called into a back room, followed by two city attorneys. Several reporters moved excitedly in and out of that room. Then, one of the reporters came over to King and handed him a news bulletin that had just come in over the Associated Press wire. "Here's the decision you've been waiting for," the reporter said.

The U.S. Supreme Court had affirmed the lower court ruling, declaring that Alabama's bus segregation laws were unconstitutional. "My heart began to throb with an inexpressible joy," King wrote later. He rushed to the back of the courtroom to tell his wife, Ralph Abernathy, and E. D. Nixon. As word of the decision spread through the courtroom, one man rose and shouted, "God Almighty has spoken from Washington, D.C.!" Judge Eugene Carter had to bang his gavel several times to restore order. Then, in an almost comic contradiction of the Supreme Court decision, Judge Carter granted a temporary injunction to ban the car pool.

The car pool would have to stop operating, but that was beside the point now. Nearly a year after the boycott had begun, the black citizens of Montgomery had won a dramatic landmark victory. Segregated seating on the buses was about to end. There would be no more rules about who could sit where. It would be so simple. Anyone would be able to sit in any vacant seat. The Supreme Court decision should not be seen as a victory of blacks over whites, King proclaimed, but as a victory for justice and democracy.

The following night, the boycotters celebrated at two enormous mass meetings, held at churches on each side of town to accommodate as many people as possible. At one meeting, the Reverend Robert Graetz was called to the pulpit for a reading of Scripture. The skinny young white preacher who had risked his family's safety by supporting the black cause opened his Bible and turned to these famous words from 1 Corinthians:

When I was a child, I spake as a child, I understood as a child, I thought as a child; but when I became a man, I put away childish things.

Before he could even finish the sentence, every single person in the church had risen to cheer the passage—a biblical affirmation of the black community's powerful new sense of pride and self-respect. "They were shouting and cheering and waving their handkerchiefs," King remembered, "as if to say they knew they had come of age, had won new dignity."

When Graetz concluded, "And now abideth faith, hope, love, but the greatest of these is love," there was another spontaneous outburst.

"I knew then that non-violence, for all its difficulties, had won its way into our hearts," King wrote.

There was one more hurdle. The Supreme Court decision would not take effect until the official court papers were issued and served on city officials. Meanwhile, bus segregation was still the law, and Judge Carter's last-minute injunction banning the car pool had already taken effect. "For these three or four days," King announced optimistically, "we will continue to walk and share rides with friends."

As it turned out, five weeks were to pass before the official legal paperwork reached Montgomery. This created a problem, since the car pool was still banned by court order. To get through the delay, a cooperative "share-a-ride" plan was worked out for each neighborhood and each street. Coordinated by the Reverend S. S. Seay, the plan worked. Car owners shared rides with friends and neighbors, while thousands of other boycotters kept on walking. The buses remained empty.

Meanwhile, boycott leaders worked to prepare people for integrated buses. During the twice-weekly mass meetings, speaker after speaker stressed the theme of nonviolence. At several meetings, training sessions were held to teach nonviolent techniques. Chairs were lined up in front of the church altar to resemble a bus, with the driver's seat in front. Then people from the audience were picked as actors to play the roles of driver and black and white passengers—some courteous, others hostile.

As the audience watched, the actors played out scenes of confrontations, episodes of insult and violence that might occur when the buses were in fact integrated. If cursed, do not curse back, black riders were advised. If pushed, do not push back. If struck, do not strike back. Exhibit love and goodwill at all times. After each scene, the actors returned to the audience and another group took their place. Each training session was followed by a general discussion.

Boycott leaders visited black schools and urged students to board the integrated buses as good citizens, calmly and with dignity, committed to absolute nonviolence. And they distributed throughout the city a mimeographed list of "Suggestions for Integrating Buses." Passengers were reminded to observe the ordinary rules of courtesy, to say "May I" or "Pardon me" as they took a vacant seat beside another rider, white or black. "If there is to be violence in word or deed," the list of suggestions advised, "it must not be our people who commit it."

On December 20, the Supreme Court's bus integration order was finally delivered to Montgomery's city officials. "I guess we'll have to abide by it," Mayor Gayle said, "because it's the law."

That evening, thousands of people gathered at the Holt Street Baptist Church, where King had electrified the crowd more than a year earlier with the speech that launched the boycott. The church was packed, and people spilled out into the street for blocks in each direction. Loudspeakers outside carried the voices of speakers and the sounds of freedom songs and spirituals through the crisp winter night air.

"We sang 'Swing Low, Sweet Chariot' and 'This Little Light of Mine, I'm Gonna Let It Shine,' and a whole lot of others," Georgia Gilmore remembered. "Weary feet and weary souls were lightened. It was such a night. We didn't have to walk no more. Even before Martin Luther King got up there and told us it was over, we knew it was over and we knew we had won."

"We must not take this as a victory," King told the crowd, "but merely with dignity. When we go back to the buses, go back with a quiet pride. Don't push your way. Just sit where there is a vacant seat. If someone pushes you, don't push back. We must have the courage to refuse to hit. . . . we must continue to resist segregation non-violently."

On December 21, 1956—381 days after the boycott began—Montgomery desegregated its public buses. At 5:55 that morning, an empty bus pulled up to the bus stop at the corner near the King home. Wearing his best suit and dress hat, Martin Luther King, Jr., walked toward the bus, accompanied by Ralph Abernathy, E. D. Nixon, and Glenn Smiley, a southern-born white minister and civil rights activist who was visiting Montgomery. Television cameras, photographers, and reporters hovered around the men, shouting questions. The bus door swung open. King stepped aboard. The white bus driver greeted him with a smile and said, "I believe you are Reverend King, aren't you."

"Yes, I am," King replied.

"We are glad to have you this morning," the driver said.

King thanked him and took a seat in the front of the bus.

King and Abernathy are among the first to ride on December 21, 1956, the day that segregated bus service ended in Montgomery. Abernathy, at left in the front seat, sits next to Inez Baskin, a reporter for the "colored page" of the Montgomery Advertiser. *King, in the seat behind Abernathy, sits next to a white minister, the Reverend Glenn Smiley of New York, who was in Montgomery as an observer. When this photo ran in newspapers around the world, Baskin was mistaken by many for Rosa Parks.*

AP/Wide World Photos

Civil rights marchers carrying a huge American flag trudge along U.S. Highway 80, named the Jefferson Davis Highway in honor of the president of the Confederacy, as they head from Selma toward the Alabama State Capitol in Montgomery, March 1965.

Library of Congress

EIGHT

THE CHILDREN COMING ON . . .

"The children coming on behind us ought to know the truth about this."

Rosa Parks never expected to make history. "I had no idea when I refused to give up my seat on that Montgomery bus that my small action would help put an end to enforced segregation in the South," she wrote many years later. In fact, no one realized it at the time, but the Montgomery bus boycott marked the beginning of what we now recognize as the modern civil rights movement.

Thousands of blacks once again rode the buses daily, though not without opposition. The White Citizens Council had predicted violence, and sure enough, violence erupted before Christmas. Early on the morning of December 23, two days after the boycott ended, a shotgun blast was fired into King's home, scaring everyone but causing no injuries. On Christmas Eve, a car pulled up to a bus stop where a fifteen-year-old black girl was standing alone. Four or five men jumped out, beat her, and drove away. Then shotgun snipers began to fire at integrated buses, sending a pregnant black woman to the hospital with bullet wounds in both legs. In response, the city commissioners suspended all bus service after 5 P.M., which meant that people who worked from nine to five couldn't ride the buses home.

In January, bombs were set off at four black churches in Montgomery

Ralph Abernathy (at right) and W. J. Hudson, a fellow minister, stand on the porch of Abernathy's home and survey the damage caused by a bomb explosion following the desegregation of Montgomery's buses, January 1957.
Library of Congress

and at the homes of three ministers—Ralph Abernathy, Robert Graetz, and Martin Luther King. The Bell Street and Mount Olive Baptist Churches were almost completely destroyed, and all three houses were severely damaged. Miraculously, no one was hurt. "Lord, I hope no one will have to die as a result of our struggle for freedom in Montgomery," King told a mass meeting.

Eventually, the sniper and bombing attacks ceased, and nighttime bus service was quietly restored. "In a few weeks transportation was back to normal," King wrote, "and people of both races rode together wherever they pleased. The skies did not fall when integrated buses finally traveled the streets of Montgomery."

As Montgomery adjusted to integrated buses, the success of the boycott proved an inspiration and a turning point. Across the South, civil rights activists, black and white, employed the power of nonviolent protests to challenge segregation on city buses, on interstate buses and trains, and at public facilities of many kinds. College students staged "sit-in demonstrations" at segregated lunch counters. Young black and white "Freedom Riders" rode buses through the South, testing a Supreme Court decision that ordered integrated facilities for all interstate passengers.

Angry segregationists, determined to stop "race mixing," fought back. Protest marches were suppressed by police using snarling German shepherds, bullwhips, and powerful fire hoses; blasted by two hundred pounds of water pressure, peaceful marchers were thrown to the pavement, swept along, and slammed against storefronts. Demonstrators were attacked by mobs, beaten, and in several instances, killed. King himself,

A seventeen-year-old civil rights demonstrator is attacked by police dogs during a protest march in Birmingham, Alabama, in May 1963.

AP/Wide World Photos

continuing his message of nonviolence, was arrested and jailed a number of times. While autographing books in a New York City department store, he was stabbed in the chest by a deranged woman who shouted, "I've been after him for six years! I'm glad I done it!"

Two violent incidents, in particular, horrified the world and stand

These four girls were killed when Ku Klux Klansmen threw a bomb into their Sunday school classroom at a Birmingham church on September 15, 1963. They are, left to right, Denise McNair, eleven; Carole Robertson, fourteen; Addie Mae Collins, fourteen; and Cynthia Wesley, fourteen.

AP/Wide World Photos

today as grisly landmarks of the civil rights movement. In Birmingham, Alabama, a powerful bomb exploded at the Sixteenth Street Baptist Church on September 15, 1963, killing four girls who were attending a Sunday school class. Years later, three Ku Klux Klan members were convicted of the bombing and sent to prison.

In Mississippi, three young civil rights workers—two white, one black—who were helping blacks register to vote disappeared near the town of Philadelphia on Sunday, June 21, 1964. After a lengthy search, their bodies were found buried under fifteen feet of earth on a nearby farm. They had been beaten to death by a mob of Klansmen. Forty-one years later, in 2005, one of the Klan members accused of the murders,

Martin Luther King, Jr., holds a photograph of three civil rights workers murdered in Mississippi in 1964: Michael Schwerner, twenty-four; James Earl Chaney, twenty-one; and Andrew Goodman, twenty.

Library of Congress

Edgar Ray Killen, was convicted of manslaughter by a local jury of blacks and whites.

During these years of protest and resistance, the civil rights movement was growing in numbers and influence, spreading to all sections of society and attracting many young people of high school and college age. In August 1963, more than 200,000 peaceful demonstrators from all over the country attended the Civil Rights March on Washington, D.C., where Martin Luther King, by then the nation's best-known civil rights leader, delivered his famous "I Have a Dream" speech from the steps of the Lincoln Memorial. "It is a dream," he said, "deeply rooted in the American dream that one day this nation will rise up and live out the true meaning of its creed—we hold these truths to be self-evident, that all men are created equal."

Continuing bloodshed and violence, meanwhile, outraged people of goodwill and resulted in mounting pressure to pass meaningful civil rights legislation. In 1963, President John F. Kennedy asked Congress to pass a federal law that would end legal segregation. Kennedy was gunned down in Dallas, Texas, in November of that year, but the bill he had requested was later passed overwhelmingly by Congress and was signed into law by President Lyndon B. Johnson as the Civil Rights Act of 1964. This landmark legislation helped transform American society. It outlawed discrimination in public facilities, such as restaurants, theaters, and hotels, in government, and in employment; it encouraged the desegregation of public schools; and it abolished the Jim Crow segregation laws in the South.

The Civil Rights Act did not guarantee the right to vote, however. That was accomplished by the Voting Rights Act, passed by Congress and signed by President Johnson in 1965, abolishing poll taxes, literacy tests, and other barriers to equal opportunity at the ballot box. Rosa Parks, Martin Luther King, Jr., and other civil rights leaders watched as President Johnson signed the act into law in the President's Room off the Capitol Rotunda, the same room where President Abraham Lincoln had signed the Emancipation Proclamation 104 years earlier.

The Voting Rights Act has been called the highest achievement of the civil rights movement. In 1964, there were only 300 black public officials nationwide. In 2005, there were more than 5,000, including 43 members of Congress. In 1975, the Voting Rights Act was expanded to include "language minorities," resulting in nearly 6,000 elected His-panic officials in 2005, including 27 in Congress.

The battle for racial equality had been going on ever since the nation's founding. It had been fought by means of lawsuits in the courts, and through political pressure in Congress and in state legislatures. And it was fought in the streets by courageous citizens who found that they could gain their rights by banding together and peacefully resisting an unjust system.

In 1968, Martin Luther King, Jr., went to Memphis, Tennessee, to support a strike by black sanitation workers who were demanding bet-ter wages and working conditions. On the evening of April 4, as King stood on the balcony of the Lorraine Motel, waiting to go to dinner, an assassin's bullet ended his life. A lone gunman, James Earl Ray, con-fessed to the killing. Many people believe that Ray, a white petty crimi-nal, did not act alone, but no conspiracy has ever been proved. King was thirty-nine. More than any other leader of his turbulent era, he had been able to give America's conscience a voice.

Other participants in the Montgomery bus boycott went on with their lives. Jo Ann Robinson resigned her position at Alabama State College, along with other faculty members who felt they were being harassed because of their political activities. Robinson moved to Cali-fornia, where she taught in the public schools for many years and remained actively engaged in civic and social work.

"Boycotting taught me courage," Robinson wrote later. "The mem-ory of thousands of boycotters, walking in hot and cold weather, in rain, sleet, and sunshine, for thirteen months, makes me feel ever so humble.

These people inspired me to refuse to accept what was wrongfully imposed upon me."

Today, Alabama State is an integrated university, part of the state of Alabama's university system.

Claudette Colvin settled in New York City. She worked as a nurse's aide and lived a quiet life in relative obscurity. Her role in the Montgomery bus boycott, ignored and almost forgotten, is recognized by several websites and by a six-minute documentary film, *Claudette Who?*, made by a group of fifth graders at Hartford University School in Milwaukee, Wisconsin.

Rosa Parks moved with her husband and mother to Detroit, where her brother lived, after receiving threatening phone calls in Montgomery. She worked for Congressman John Conyers, continued to campaign for equal rights, and was celebrated as the "Mother of the Civil Rights Movement."

In 1995, when Parks visited Alabama to observe the fortieth anniversary of the bus boycott, siren-blaring motorcycle cops stopped traffic for her. The mayor of Birmingham proclaimed "Rosa Parks Day." The mayor of Montgomery presented the eighty-two-year-old civil rights veteran with the key to the city. And the Montgomery City Council, made up of four black and five white members, announced plans for the Rosa Parks Library and Museum, which was dedicated in Montgomery in December, 2000. "I'd like for everybody to remember me as a person who wanted to be free," Parks said. She died, aged ninety-two, at her Detroit home on October 24, 2005—six weeks before the fiftieth anniversary of the beginning of the Montgomery bus boycott.

Rosa Parks sits up front on a newly integrated Montgomery bus, December 26, 1956.

Photo by Don Cravens/Getty Images

Parks's defiance on that December evening in 1955 set in motion a peaceful revolution that led to the death of Jim Crow segregation in the South and brought black Americans into the nation's political life. But the success and true impact of the Montgomery boycott depended on the sacrifices and determination of thousands whose names are lost to history—maids, laborers, teachers, students, cooks, and others—ordinary people who rose above the safe routines of their daily lives to become actors in an historical drama that changed a nation.

E. D. Nixon remained a lifelong railroad man and a spirited civic leader in Montgomery. "The Montgomery boycott was a big thing in a whole lot of people's lives," he remembered. "There are hundreds of people who made a contribution. The children coming on behind us ought to know the truth about this. The truth will set you free."

CHAPTER NOTES

The following notes refer to the sources of quoted material. Each citation includes the first and last words or phrases of the quotation and the source. Unless otherwise noted, references are to works cited in the Selected Bibliography, beginning on page 108.

Abbreviations used are:

Branch–Taylor Branch, *Parting the Waters*

Eyes–Juan Williams, *Eyes on the Prize*

Fifties–David Halberstam, *The Fifties*

Gray–Fred Gray, *Bus Ride to Justice*

JAR–Jo Ann Robinson, *The Montgomery Bus Boycott and the Women Who Started It*

Leventhal–Willy S. Leventhal, *The Children Coming On . . .*

Levine–Ellen Levine, *Freedom's Children*

MLK–Martin Luther King, Jr., *Stride Toward Freedom*

Parks–Rosa Parks/Jim Haskins, *My Story*

ONE JO ANN ROBINSON

Selma-to-Montgomery civil rights marchers wave American flags in front of the Alabama State Capitol at the end of their five-day march, 1965.

Library of Congress

10   "better seating . . . such an idea!": JAR, p. 23
12   "Mayor Gayle . . . boycott of buses": Eyes, p. 62
      "I did not . . . bus company": JAR, p. 27

two CLAUDETTE COLVIN

Page

16   "Hey, get up! . . . the cops": Levine, p. 23
      "Aren't you . . . constitutional right!" Levine, p. 24
      "You have . . . do this": Levine, p. 24
16–17 "I didn't know . . . helpless": Levine, p. 25

17   "She insisted . . . white": Fifties, p. 546

20   "The verdict . . . ever been": JAR, p. 42

21   "I had . . . bus line": Eyes, p. 63

        "[The driver] asked . . . anybody else does": Leventhal, p. 152

THREE ROSA PARKS

Page

23   "where you . . . treated": Parks, p. 107

24–25   "I was . . . cotton": Parks, p. 35

25   "But that still . . . diploma": Parks, p. 65

        "That was . . . up there": Eyes, p. 66

27   "Let me . . . have those seats": Parks, p. 115

        "But that . . . giving in": Parks, p. 116

28   "Look, woman . . . stand up?": Fifties, p. 540

        "No, I'm not . . . arrested": Eyes, p. 66

        "You may do that . . . beaten": Parks, p. 116

        "Why do you . . . under arrest": Parks, p. 117

        "I'm in jail . . . in jail": Parks, p. 121

30   "none of . . . business": Branch, p. 129

30–31   "Mrs. Durr . . . sisters": Parks, p. 122

31   "Mrs. Parks . . . case": Eyes, p. 62

        "Oh, the white . . . kill you": Fifties, p. 543

33   "I decided . . . Alabama": Leventhal, p. 91

        "If you think . . . with it": Branch, p. 131

        "It was . . . Bus Boycott": Gray, p. 52

34–35   "Another Negro . . . Monday": Leventhal, p. 99

FOUR MARTIN LUTHER KING, JR.

Page

36   "Don't ride . . . walk": MLK, p. 48

37   "PEOPLE . . . FREEDOM": Eyes, p. 72

       "I was . . . Montgomery": MLK, p. 53

38   "By this time . . . jubilant": MLK, p. 54

39   "protect Negro riders": JAR, p. 57

40   "Negro goon squads": JAR, p. 57

40–41 "If there . . . faint-hearted few": JAR, p. 58

41   "The few . . . various stops": Eyes, p. 73

       "The trial . . . on the other": Gray, pp. 55–56

42   "They never . . . fired her": Leventhal, p. 89

       "Let me . . . a coward": Branch, p. 136, and Fifties, p. 547

43   "The [vote] . . . nomination": MLK, p. 56

43–44 "Reverend King . . . kind of thing": Eyes, p. 73

44   "I had come . . . freedom": MLK, p. 85

       "The church . . . was happening": Eyes, p. 71

45   "The Holt Street . . . master speaker": Eyes, p. 74

       "the most decisive . . . inadequacy": MLK, p. 59

       "determined to apply . . . means": Branch, p. 139

45–46 "But there comes . . . oppression": MLK, p. 61

46–47 "Now let us . . . protest": Branch, p. 140

47   "In our protest . . . intimidation": MLK, p. 62

       "We are not . . . stream!": Branch, p. 140

       "If you . . . responsibility": MLK, p. 63

       "All in favor . . . stand": MLK, p. 64

       "Comes the first . . . buses": Fifties, p. 556

FIVE BOYCOTT HEROES

Young members of the Washington Freedom Riders Committee set out from New York City on their way to Washington, D.C., to protest segregation, 1961. Freedom riders usually worked in interracial teams; some were attacked by mobs of Klansmen and savagely beaten when their buses crossed into the Deep South.
Library of Congress

six PROUD TO BE ARRESTED

Page

59   "a very pleasant . . . with us": JAR, p. 25

59–61 "There seems . . . commissioners": Eyes, pp. 81 and 85

61   "If the mayor . . . maid": Parks, p. 145

62   "a group . . . radicals": Eyes, p. 81

63   "Get out . . . with the others": MLK, pp. 128–129, and Branch, p. 160

        "For the first . . . bars": MLK, p. 189

64   "get out . . . else": MLK, p. 132

        "Listen, nigger . . . Montgomery": MLK, p. 134, and Branch, p. 162

        "that many . . . to me": MLK, p. 133

        "With my head . . . anything": MLK, pp. 184–185

66   "this unfortunate . . . city": MLK, p. 132

        "Regrets . . . policy": MLK, p. 137, and Branch, p. 165

        "Let's not . . . love": MLK, p. 137, and Branch, p. 166

        "Let us hear the commissioner": MLK, p. 138

67   "Nonviolence . . . tests": MLK, p. 140

        "I kept . . . to me": JAR, p. 140

        "without . . . excuse": Branch, p. 168

        "We have walked . . . city fathers": Branch, p. 173

69   "I say . . . jail!": Branch, p. 173

        "They are . . . you": MLK, p. 144

        "I must . . . away": MLK, p. 145

        "They're going . . . my boy": Fifties, p. 562

        "Are you . . . I am": Branch, p. 176

71   "This is . . . experiences": JAR, p. 154

        "This is no vaudeville show!": Branch, p. 177

SEVEN WALKING TO VICTORY

Page

EIGHT THE CHILDREN COMING ON . . .

Page

89   "I had . . . South": Parks, p. 2

91   "Lord, I hope . . . Montgomery": Branch, p. 201

        "In a few . . . Montgomery": MLK, p. 180

92   "I've been . . . done it!": Branch, p. 243

94–95   "It is a dream . . . created equal": *The Young Reader's Companion to American History*, edited by John A. Garraty (Boston: Houghton Mifflin, 1994), p. 472

96–97   "Boycotting taught . . . upon me": JAR, p. 3

97   "I'd like . . . to be free": "A Person Who Wanted to Be Free," *Washington Post Magazine*, October 3, 1995, p. 29

99   "The Montgomery boycott . . . set you free": Leventhal, p. 22

SELECTED BIBLIOGRAPHY

As a seminal event that spearheaded the modern American civil rights movement, and as a dramatic story with a beginning, a middle, and a triumphant ending, the Montgomery bus boycott has been the subject of numerous histories, memoirs, articles, monographs, and dissertations. For my account, I have focused on the first-hand recollections of several significant participants in the boycott, as recorded in the following books:

The Montgomery Bus Boycott and the Women Who Started It: The Memoir of Jo Ann Gibson Robinson, edited with a foreword by David J. Garrow (Knoxville: University of Tennessee Press, 1987). Robinson's autobiographical account of the creation of the boycott emphasizes the crucial role played by the Women's Political Council.

Rosa Parks: My Story, by Rosa Parks with Jim Haskins (New York: Dial, 1992). Also published as a Puffin Books paperback for young readers, this is an inspiring autobiography for all ages.

Stride Toward Freedom: The Montgomery Story, by Martin Luther King, Jr. (New York: Harper & Row, 1958). King's first book, his personal account of the boycott and the evolving application of nonviolent resistance in America. Also published in an edition for young readers (New York: HarperCollins Children's Books, 1987).

Bus Ride to Justice: The Life and Works of Fred Gray, by Fred Gray (Montgomery, Ala.: Black Belt Press, 1995; NewSouth Books, 2002). The boycott story as told by the attorney at the time for Rosa Parks and Martin Luther King, Jr. Gray's autobiography also details his later work as a civil rights lawyer representing the Freedom Riders, the Selma-to-Montgomery marchers, and others.

The Children Coming On . . . : A Retrospective of the Montgomery Bus Boycott, edited by Willy S. Leventhal et al. (Montgomery, Ala.: Black Belt Press, 1998). An invaluable compendium of essays, interviews, oral histories, court documents, and news clippings.

Freedom's Children: Young Civil Rights Activists Tell Their Own Stories, by Ellen Levine

An employee of the Dallas, Texas, Transit Company removes a sign requiring segregated seating from the rear of a bus after the company announced it was ending passenger segregation on all of its 530 buses.

Library of Congress

(New York: G. P. Putnam's Sons, 1993; Puffin, 2000). Includes interviews with Claudette Colvin and twenty-nine other African Americans who were children or teenagers in the 1950s and 1960s.

Outstanding historical narratives include:

Parting the Waters: America in the King Years, 1954–63, by Taylor Branch (New York: Simon & Schuster, 1988). Winner of the Pulitzer Prize, this is the definitive account of the American civil rights movement and an indispensible source for anyone writing on this topic.

The Fifties, by David Halberstam (New York: Villard, 1993). Offers a sweeping narrative history of the decade that saw the beginnings of the civil rights movement.

Eyes on the Prize: America's Civil Rights Years, 1954–1965, by Juan Williams (New York: Viking Penguin, 1987). Published as a companion to the six-part PBS television series, this book combines written and oral sources with an historical overview of the period.

Other books about the Montgomery bus boycott include:

Daybreak of Freedom: The Montgomery Bus Boycott, edited by Stewart Burns (Chapel Hill: University of North Carolina Press, 1997); *The Walking City: The Montgomery Bus Boycott, 1955–1956*, edited with a preface by David J. Garrow (Brooklyn, N.Y.: Carlson Publishing, 1989); *A White Preacher's Memoir: The Montgomery Bus Boycott*, by Robert S. Graetz (Montgomery, Ala.: Black Belt Press, 1998); *The Birth of the Montgomery Bus Boycott*, by Roberta Hughes Wright (Southfield, Mich.: Charro Press, 1991).

Rosa Parks, by Douglas Brinkley (New York: Viking, 2000), part of the Penguin Lives series, provides a short but scholarly account of Parks's personality and her political life in the South and in Detroit before and after the Montgomery bus boycott. *Martin Luther King, Jr.*, by Marshall Frady (New York: Viking, 2002), another volume in the Penguin Lives series, offers an insightful biographical portrait of King.

Books for young readers include:

Getting Away With Murder: The True Story of the Emmett Till Case, by Chris Crowe (New York: Dial, 2003); *A Dream of Freedom: The Civil Rights Movement From 1954 to 1968*, by Diane McWhorter (New York: Scholastic, 2004); *There Comes a Time: The Struggle for Civil Rights*, by Milton Meltzer (New York: Random House, 2001); *I've Seen the Promised Land: The Life of Dr. Martin Luther King, Jr.*, by Walter Dean Myers (New York: HarperCollins, 2004); *Witnesses to Freedom: Young People Who Fought for Civil Rights*, by Belinda Rochelle (New York: Lodestar Books/Dutton, 1993; Puffin, 1997).

Websites devoted to the Montgomery bus boycott and to many of its participants can be accessed by searching the Internet for "Rosa Parks," "Dr. Martin Luther King, Jr.," "Claudette Colvin," "Clifford and Virginia Durr," "Robert Graetz," "E. D. Nixon," "Jo Ann Robinson," and others, as well as "Montgomery bus boycott."

ACKNOWLEDGMENTS

For their advice and many kindnesses while I was researching this book, I am grateful to E. Ann Clemons, manager of the Montgomery Convention and Visitor Bureau; Georgette M. Norman, director of the Rosa Parks Library and Museum in Montgomery; Dr. Gwendolyn M. Patton, archivist at Trenholm State Technical College, Montgomery; and Dr. Howard Robinson, director of the African American Center at Alabama State University, Montgomery.

My thanks to the following for their help in obtaining photographs: John Broderick and Sandra Weiner; Joan Carroll at Wide World Photos; Iris Wong at Getty Images; and the staff at the Prints and Photographs Reading Room, Library of Congress.

INDEX

Page numbers in *italics* refer to illustrations and captions.